The Poetry of Laurence Binyon

Volume XII - The Cause – Poems of the War

Robert Laurence Binyon, CH, was born on August 10th, 1869 in Lancaster in Lancashire, England to Quaker parents, Frederick Binyon and Mary Dockray.

He studied at St Paul's School, London before enrolling at Trinity College, Oxford, to read classics.

Binyon's first published work was Persephone in 1890. As a poet, his output was not prodigious and, in the main, the volumes he did publish were slim. But his reputation was of the highest order. When the Poet Laureate, Alfred Austin, died in 1913, Binyon was considered alongside Thomas Hardy and Rudyard Kipling for the post which was given to Robert Bridges.

Binyon played a pivotal role in helping to establish the modernist School of poetry and introduced imagist poets such as Ezra Pound, Richard Aldington and H.D. (Hilda Doolittle) to East Asian visual art and literature. Most of his career was spent at The British Museum where he produced many books particularly centering on the art of the Far East.

Moved and shaken by the onset of the World War I and its military tactics of young men slaughtered to hold or gain a few yards of shell-shocked mud Binyon wrote his seminal poem *For the Fallen*. It became an instant classic, turning moments of great loss into a National and human tribute.

After the war, he returned to the British Museum and wrote numerous books on art; especially on William Blake, Persian and Japanese art.

In 1931, his two volume Collected Poems appeared and in 1933, he retired from the British Museum.

Between 1933 and 1943, Binyon published his acclaimed translation of Dante's *Divine Comedy* in an English version of terza rima.

During the Second World War Binyon wrote another poetic masterpiece *'The Burning of the Leaves'*, about the London Blitz.

Robert Laurence Binyon died in Dunedin Nursing Home, Bath Road, Reading, on March 10th, 1943 after undergoing an operation.

Index of Contents

PRELUDES

EUROPE, MDCCCCI

TO NAPOLEON

Soars still thy spirit, Child of Fire?
Dost hear the camps of Europe hum?
On eagle wings dost hover nigher
At the far rolling of the drum?

To see the harvest thou hast sown
Smilest thou now, Napoleon?

Long had the world in blinded mirth
Or suffering patience dreamed content,
When lo! like thunder over earth
Thy challenge pealed, the skies were rent:
Thy terrible youth rose up alone
Against the old world on its throne.

With shuddering then the peoples gazed,
And such a stupor bound them dumb
As those fierce Colchian ranks amazed
Who saw the youthful Jason come,
And challenging the War God's name
Step forth, his fiery yoke to tame.

He took those dread bulls by the horn,
Harnessed their fury to his will,
And in the furrow swiftly torn
The dragon's teeth abroad did spill:
Behold, behind his trampling heel
The furrow flowered into steel!

A spear, a plume, a warrior sprung —
Armed gods in wrath by hundreds; he
Faced all, and full amidst them flung
His magic helmet: instantly
Their swords upon themselves they drew,
And shouting each the other slew.

But no Medean spell was thine,
Napoleon, nor anointed charm;
Thy will was as a fate divine
To wavering men who watched thine arm
Drive on through Europe old thy plough.
The harvest ripens even now!

Time's purple flauntings, king and crown,
Old custom's tall and idle weeds,
Were tossed aside and trampled down,
While thou didst scatter fiery seeds,
That in the gendering lap of earth
Prepared a new world's Titan birth.

Then in thy path from underground,
Where long benumbed in trance they froze,
The Nations, giant forms unbound,

Slow to their aching stature rose;
And through their wintry veins again
Slow flushed the streams of life in pain.

Thy thunder, O Napoleon, passed;
But these whom thou hadst stirred to life,
On them the imperious doom was cast
Of inextinguishable strife.
For peace they long, but blood and tears
Still blinded the tempestuous years.

A hundred years have flown, and still
For peace they pine; peace tarries yet.
These groaning armies Europe fill,
And war's red planet hath not set.
O mockery <of peace, that gnaws
Their hearts for so abhorred a cause!

Is peace so easy? Nay, the names
That are most dear and most divine
To men, are like the heavenly flames
That farthest from possession shine.
Peace, love, truth, freedom, unto these
The way is through the storming seas.

Ye wakened Nations, now no more
You battle for a monarch's whim;
The cause is now in your heart's core,
Your soul must strive through every limb;
They who with all their soul contend
Bear more, but to a nobler end.

Be patient in your strife! And thou,
O England, dearer than the rest;
England, with proud looks on thy brow,
England, with trouble at thy breast,
Seek on in patient fortitude
Strong peace, most worthy to be wooed.

Take up thy task, O nobly born!
With both hands grasp thy destiny.
Easy is ignorance, easy scorn,
And fluent pride, unworthy thee.
Grand rolls the planet of thy fate:
Be thy just passions also great!

Turn from the sweet lure of content,
Rise up among the courts of ease;

Be all thy will as a bow bent,
Thy sure oncoming like thy seas.
Purge clear within thy deep desires
To be our burning altar-fires!

Then welcome peril, so it bring
Thy true soul leaping into light;
A glory for our mouths to sing
And for our deeds to match in might,
Till thou at last our hope enthrone
And make indeed thy peace our own.

January 1901

THE BELFRY OF BRUGES

Keen comes the dizzy air
In one tumultuous breath.
The tower to heaven lies bare;
Dumb stir the streets beneath.

Immeasurable sky
Domes upward from the dim
Round land, the astonished eye
Supposes the world's rim.

And through the sea of space
Winds drive the furious cloud
Silent in endless race;
And the tower rocks aloud.

Mine eye now wanders wide,
My thought now quickens keen.
O cities, far descried,
What ravage have you seen

Of an enkindled world?
Homes blazing and hearths bare;
Of hosts tyrannic hurled
On pale ranks of despair,

Who fed with warm proud blood
The cause unquenchable,
For which your heroes stood,
For which our Sidney fell;

Sidney, whose starry fame,
Mirrored in noble song,
Shines, all our sloth to shame,
And arms us against wrong;

Bright star, that seems to burn
Over yon English shore,
Whither my feet return,
And my thoughts run before;

Run with this rumour brought
By the wild wind's alarms,
Dark sounds with battle fraught,
Menace of distant arms.

O menace harsh, but vain t
For what can peril do
But search our souls again
To sift and find the true?

Prove if the sap of old
Shoots yet from the old seed,
If faith be still unsold,
If truth be truth indeed?

Welcome the blast that shakes
The wall wherein we have lain
Slumbering, our heart awakes
And rends the prison chain.

Turn we from prosperous toys
And the dull name of ease;
Rather than tarnished joys
Face we the angry seas!

Or if old age infirm
Be in our veins congealed,
Bow we to Time, our term
Fulfilled, and proudly yield.

Not each to each we are made,
Not each to each we fall,
But every true part played
Quickens the heart of all

That feeds and moves and fires
The many-peopled lands,
And in our languor tires

But in our strength expands.

For forward-gazing eyes
Fate shall no terror keep.
She in our own breast lies:
Now let her wake from sleep!

1898

THUNDER ON THE DOWNS

Wide earth, wide heaven, and in the summer air
Silence! The summit of the Down is bare
Between the climbing crests of wood; but those
Great sea-winds, wont, when the wet South-West blows,
To rock tall beeches and strong oaks aloud
And strew torn leaves upon the streaming cloud
To-day are idle, slumbering far aloof.
Under the solemn height and gorgeous roof
Of cloud-built sky, all earth is indolent.
Wandering hum of bees and thymy scent
Of the short turf enrich pure loneliness;
Scarcely an airy topmost-twining tress
Of bryony quivers where the thorn it wreathes;
Hot fragrance from the honeysuckle breathes;
And sweet the rose floats on the arching brier's
Green fountain, sprayed with delicate frail fires.

For clumps of thicket, dark beneath the blaze
Of the high westering sun, beset the ways
Of smooth grass narrowing where the slope runs steep
Down to green woods, and glowing shadows keep
A freshness round the mossy roots, and cool
The light that sleeps as in a chequered pool
Of golden air. O woods, I love you well,
I love the flowers you hide, your ferny smell;
But here is sweeter solitude, for here
My heart breathes heavenly space; the sky is near
To thought, with heights that fathomlessly glow;
And the eye wanders the wide land below.

And this is England! June's undarkened green
Gleams on far woods; and in the vales between
Grey hamlets, older than the trees that shade
Their ripening meadows, are in quiet laid,
Themselves a part of the warm, fruitful ground.

The little hills of England rise around;

The little streams that wander from them shine
And with their names remembered names entwine
Of old renown and honour, fields of blood
High causes fought on, stubborn hardihood
For freedom spent, and songs, our noblest pride,
That in the heart of England never died
And, burning still, make splendour of our tongue.
Glories enacted, spoken, suffered, sung!
You lie emblazoned on this land now sleeping;
And southward, over leagues of forest sweeping
White on the verge glistens the famous sea,
That English wave, on which so haughtily
Towered her sails, and one sail homeward bore
Past capes of silently lamenting shore
Victory's dearest dead. O shores of home,
Since by the vanished watch-fire shields of Rome
Dinted this upland turf, what hearts have ached
To see you far away, what eyes have waked
Ere dawn to watch those cliffs of long desire
One after one rise in their voiceless choir
Out of the twilight over the rough blue
Like music! . . .

But now heavy gleams imbrue
The inland air. Breathless the valleys hold
Their colours in a veil of sultry gold
With mingled shadows that have ceased to crawl;
For far in heaven is thunder! Over all
A single cloud in slow magnificence
Climbs like a mountain, gradual and immense,
With awful head unstirring, and moved on
Against the zenith, towers above the sun.
And still it thickens luminous fold on fold
Of fatal colour, ominously scrolled
And fleeced with fire; above the sun it towers
Like some vast thought quickening a world not ours
Remote in the waste blue, as if behind
Its rim were splendour that could smite us blind,
So doom-piled and intense it crests heaven's height
And mounting makes a menace of the light.

A menace! Yes, for when light comes, we fear.
Light that may touch, as the pure angel-spear,
Us to ourselves, make visible, make start
The apparition of the very heart
And mystery of our thoughts, awaked from under

The mask of cheating habit, and to thunder
Bare in a moment of white fire what we
Have feared and fled, our own reality.

And if a lightning now were loosed in flame
Out of the darkness of the cloud to claim
Thy heart, O England, how wouldst thou be known
In that hour? How to the quick core be shown
And seen? What cry should from thy very soul
Answer the judgment of that thunder-roll?

I hear a voice arraign thee. "Where is now
The exaltation that once lit thy brow?
Thou countest all thy ocean-sundered lands,
Thou heapest up the labours of thy hands,
Thou seest all thy ships upon the seas.
But in thine own heart mean idolatries

Usurp devotion, choke thee and annul
Noble excess of spirit, and make dull
Thine eyes, enfleshed with much dominion.
Art thou so great and is the glory gone?
Do these bespeak thy freedom who deflower
Time, and make barren every senseless hour,
Who from themselves hurry, like men afraid
Lest what they are be to themselves betrayed?
Or those who in their huddled thousands sweat
To buy the sleep that helps them to forget? —
Life lies unused, life in its loveliness!
While the cry ravens still, ' Possess, Possess!'
And there is no possession. All the lust
Of gainful man is quieted in dust;
His faith, his fear, his joy, his doom he owns,
No more: the rest is parcelled with his bones
Save what the imagination of his heart
Can to the labour of his hands impart,
Making stones serve his spirit's desire, and breathe.
But thou, what dost thou to the world bequeath,
Who gatherest riches in a waste of mind
Unto what end, O confidently blind,
Forgetful of the things that grow not old
And alone live and are not bought or sold!"

Speaks that voice truth? Is it for this that great
And tender spirits suffered scorn and hate,
Loved to the utmost, poured themselves, gave all
Nor counted cost, spirits imperial?
Where are they now, they that our memory guard

Among the nations? Shall I say, enstarred
And throned aloof? No, not from heavens of thought
Watching our muddied brief procession, not
Judges sublime above us, without share
In our thronged ways of struggle, hope, despair,
But in our blood, our dreams, our deeds they stir,
Strive on our lips for language, shame and spur
The sluggard in us, out of darkness come
Like summoned champions when the world is dumb;
Within our hearts they wait with all they gave:
Woe to us, woe, if we become their grave!

It shall not be. Darken thy pall, and trail,
Thunder of heaven, above the valleys pale!
Another England in my vision glows.
And she is armed within; at last she knows
Herself, and what to her own soul belongs.
Mid the world's irremediable wrongs
She keeps her faith; and nothing of her name
Or of her handiwork but doth proclaim
Her purpose. Her own soul hath made her free,
Not circumstance; she knows no victory
Save of the mind: in her is nothing done,
No wrong, no shame, no glory of any one,
But is the cause of all and each, a thing
Felt like a fire to kindle and to sting
The proud blood of a nation. On her brows
Is hope; her body doth her spirit house
Express and eloquent, not numb and frore;
And her voice echoes over sea and shore,
And all the lands and isles that are her own
In choric interchange and antiphon
Answer, as fancy hears in yonder cloud
From vale to vale repeated low and loud
The still-suspended thunder.

Hearts of Youth,
High-beating, ardent, quick in hope and ruth
And noble anger, O wherever now
You dedicate your uncorrupted vow
To be an energy of Light, a sword
Of the ever-living Will, amid abhorred
Din of the reeking street and populous den
Where under the great stars blind lusts of men
War on each other, or escaped to hills
Where peace the solitary evening fills,
Or far remote on other soils of earth
Keeping the dearness of your fathers' hearth

On vast plains of the West, or Austral strands
Of the warm under-world, or storied lands
Of the orient sun, or over ocean ways
Stemming the wave through blue or stormy days,
Wherever, as the circling light slopes round,
On human lips is heard an English sound,
O scattered, silent, hidden and unknown,
Be lifted up, for you are not alone!
High-beating hearts, to your deep vows be true!
Live out your dreams, for England lives in you.

Midsummer 1911

THE FOURTH OF AUGUST

Now in thy splendour go before us,
Spirit of England, ardent-eyed,
Enkindle this dear earth that bore us,
In the hour of peril purified.

The cares we hugged drop out of vision;
Our hearts with deeper thoughts dilate.
We step from days of sour division
Into the grandeur of our fate.

For us the glorious dead have striven,
They battled that we might be free.
We to their living cause are given;
We arm for men that are to be.

Among the nations nobliest chartered,
England recalls her heritage.
In her is that which is not bartered,
Which force can neither quell nor cage.

For her immortal stars are burning,
With her the hope that's never done,
The seed that's in the Spring's returning,
The very flower that seeks the sun.

She fights the fraud that feeds desire on
Lies, in a lust to enslave or kill,
The barren creed of blood and iron,
Vampire of Europe's wasted will . . .

Endure, O Earth! and thou, awaken,
Purged by this dreadful winnowing-fan,
O wronged, untameable, unshaken
Soul of divinely suffering man.

ODE FOR SEPTEMBER

I

On that long day when England held her breath,
Suddenly gripped at heart
And called to choose her part
Between her loyal soul and luring sophistries,
We watched the wide, green-bosomed land beneath
Driven and tumultuous skies;
We watched the volley of white shower after shower
Desolate with fierce drops the fallen flower;
'And still the rain's retreat
Drew glory on its track,
And still, when all was darkness and defeat,
Upon dissolving cloud the bow of peace shone back.
So in our hearts was alternating beat,
With very dread elate;
And Earth dyed all her day in colours of our fate.

II

But oh, how faint the image we foretold
In fancies of our fear
Now that the truth is here!
And we awake from dream yet think it still a dream.
It bursts our thoughts with more than thought can hold;
And more than human seem
These agonies of conflict; Elements
At war! yet not with vast indifference
Casually crushing; nay,
It is as if were hurled
Lightnings that murdered, seeking out their prey;
As if an earthquake shook to chaos half the world,
Equal in purpose as in power to slay;
And thunder stunned our ears
Streaming in rain of blood on torrents that are tears.

III

Around a planet rolls the drum's alarm.
Far where the summer smiles
Upon the utmost isles,
Danger is treading silent as a fever-breath.
Now in the North the secret waters arm;
Under the wave is Death:
They fight in the very air, the virgin air,
Hovering on fierce wings to the onset: there
Nations to battle stream;
Earth smokes and cities burn;
Heaven thickens in a storm of shells that scream;
The long lines shattering break, turn and again return;
And still across a continent they teem,
Moving in myriads; more
Than ranks of flesh and blood, but soul with soul at war!

IV

All the hells are awake: the old serpents hiss
From dungeons of the mind;
Fury of hate born blind,
Madness and lust, despairs and treacheries unclean;
They shudder up from man's most dark abyss.
But there are heavens serene
That answer strength with strength; they stand secure;
They arm us from within, and we endure.
Now are the brave more brave,
Now is the cause more dear,
The more the tempests of the darkness rave,
As, when the sun goes down, the shining stars are clear.
Radiant the spirit rushes to the grave.
Glorious it is to live
In such an hour, but life is lovelier yet to give.

V

Alas! what comfort for the uncomforted,
Who knew no cause, nor sought
Glory or gain? they are taught,
Homeless in homes that burn, what human hearts can bear.
The children stumble over their dear dead,
Wandering they know not where.
And there is one who simply fights, obeys,
Tramps, till he loses count of nights and days,

Tired, mired in dust and sweat,
Far from his own hearth-stone;
A common man of common earth, and yet
The battle-winner he, a man of no renown,
Where "food for cannon" pays a nation's debt
This is Earth's hero, whom
The pride of Empire tosses careless to his doom.

VI

Now will we speak, while we have eyes for tears
And fibres to be wrung
And in our mouths a tongue.
We will bear wrongs untold but will not only bear;
Not only bear, but build through striving years
The answer of our prayer,
That whatsoever has the noble name
Of man, shall not be yoked to alien shame;
That life shall be indeed
Life, not permitted breath
Of spirits wrenched and forced to others' need,
Robbed of their nature's joy and free alone in death.
The world shall travail in that cause, shall bleed,
But deep in hope it dwells
Until the morning break which the long night foretells.

VII

O children filled with your own airy glee
Or with a grief that comes
So swift, so strange, it numbs,
If on your growing youth this page of terror bite,
Harden not then your senses, feel and be
The promise of the light.
O heirs of Man, keep in your hearts not less
The divine torrents of his tenderness!
'T is ever war: but rust
Grows on the sword; the tale
Of earth is strewn with empires heaped in dust
Because they dreamed that force should punish and prevail.
The will to kindness lives beyond their lust;
Their grandeurs are undone:
Deep, deep within man's soul are all his victories won.

THE ANTAGONISTS

I

Caverns mouthed with blackness more than night,
Fever-jungle deep in strangling brier,
Venom-breeding slime that loathest light,
Who has plumbed your secret? who the blind desire
Hissing from the viper's lifted jaws,
Maddening the beast with scent of prey
Tracked through savage glooms on robber paws
Till the slaughter gluts him red and reeking?

Nay,
Man, this breathing mystery, this intense
Body beautiful with thinking eyes,
Master of a spirit outsoaring sense,
Spirit of tears and laughter, who has measured all the skies, —
Is he also the lair
Of a lust, of a sting
That hides from the air
Yet is lurking to spring
From the nescient core
Of his fibre, alert
At the trumpet of war
And hungry to hurt,
When he hears from abysses of time
Aboriginal mutters, replying
To something he knew not within him,
And the Demon of Earth crying:

"I am the will of the Fire
That bursts into boundless fury;
I am my own implacable desire.

"I am the will of the Sea
That shoulders the ships and breaks them;
There is none other but me."

Heavy forests bred them,
The race that dreamed.
In the bones of savage earth
Their dreams had birth:
Darkness fed them.
And the full brain grossly teemed
With thoughts compressed, with rages
Obstinate, stark, obscure —
Thirsts no time assuages,

But centuries immure.
As the sap of trees, behind
Crumpled bark of bossy boles,
Presses up its juices blind,
Buried within their souls
The dream insatiate still
Nursed its fierceness old
And violent will,
Haunted with twilight where the Gods drink full
Ere they renew their revelry of slaying,
And warriors leap like the lion on the bull,
And harsh horns in the northern mist are braying.
Tenebrous in them lay the dream
Like a fire that under ashes
Smoulders heavy-heaped and dim
Yet with spurted stealthy flashes
Sends a goblin shadow floating
Crooked on the rafters — then
Sudden from its den
Springs in splendour. So should burst
Destiny from dream, from thirst
Rapture gloating
On a vision of earth afar
Stretched for a prize and a prey;
And the secular might of the Gods re-risen
Savage and glorious, waiting its day,
Should shatter its ancient prison
And leap like the panther to slay,
Magnificent! Storm, then, and thunder
The haughty to crush with the tame,
For the world is the strong man's plunder
Whose coming is swifter than flame;
And the nations unready, decayed,
Unworthy of fate or afraid,
Shall be stricken and torn asunder
Or yield in shame.

The Dream is fulfilled.
Is it this that you willed,
O patient ones?
For this that you gave
Young to the grave
Your valiant sons?
For this that you wore
Brave faces, and bore
The burden heart-breaking —
Sublimely deceived,
You that bled and believed —

For the Dream? or the Waking?

II

No drum-beat, pulsing challenge and desire,
Sounded, no jubilant boast nor fierce alarm
Cried throbbing from enfevered throats afire
For glory, when from vineyard, forge, and farm,
From wharf and warehouse, foundry, shop, and school,
From the unreaped cornfield and the office-stool
France called her sons; but loth, but grave,
But silent, with their purpose proud and hard
Within them, as of men that go to guard
More than life, yet to dare
More than death: France, it was their France to save!
Nor now the fiery legend of old fames
And that imperial Eagle whose wide wings
Hovered from Vistula to Finistère,
Who plucked the crown from Kings,
Filled her; but France was arming in her mind:
The world unborn and helpless, not the past
Victorious with banners, called her on;
And she assembled not her sons alone
From city and hamlet, coast and heath and hill,
But deep within her bosom, deeper still
Than any fear could search, than any hope could blind,
Beyond all clamours of her recent day,
Hot smouldering of the faction and the fray,
She summoned her own soul. In the hour of night,
In the hush that felt the armed tread of her foes,
Like a star, silent out of seas, it rose.

Most human France! In those clear eyes of light
Was vision of the issue, and all the cost
To the last drop of generous blood, the last
Tears of the orphan and the widow; and yet
She shrank not from the terror of the debt,
Seeing what else were with the cause undone,
The very skies barred with an iron threat,
The very mind of freedom lost
Beneath that shadow bulked across the sun.
Therefore did she abstain
From all that had renowned her, all that won
The world's delight: thought-stilled
With deep reality to the heart she burned,
And took upon her all the load of pain
Foreknown; and her sons turned

From wife's and children's kiss
Simply, and steady-willed
With quiet eyes, with courage keen and clear,
Faced Eastward. — If an English voice she hear,
That has no speech worthy of her, let this
Be of that day remembered, with what pride
Our ancient island thrilled to the oceans wide,
And our hearts leapt to know that England then,
Equal in faith of free and loyal men,
Stept to her side.

TO WOMEN

Your hearts are lifted up, your hearts
That have foreknown the utter price.
Your hearts burn upward like a flame
Of splendour and of sacrifice.

For you, you too, to battle go,
Not with the marching drums and cheers
But in the watch of solitude
And through the boundless night of fears.

Swift, swifter than those hawks of war,
Those threatening wings that pulse the air,
Far as the vanward ranks are set,
You are gone before them, you are there!

And not a shot comes blind with death
And not a stab of steel is pressed
Home, but invisibly it tore
And entered first a woman's breast.

Amid the thunder of the guns,
The lightnings of the lance and sword
Your hope, your dread, your throbbing pride,
Your infinite passion is outpoured

From hearts that are as one high heart
Withholding naught from doom and bale,
Burningly offered up, — to bleed,
To bear, to break, but not to fail!

FOR THE FALLEN

With proud thanksgiving, a mother for her children,
England mourns for her dead across the sea.
Flesh of her flesh they were, spirit of her spirit,
Fallen in the cause of the free.

Solemn the drums thrill: Death august and royal
Sings sorrow up into immortal spheres.
There is music in the midst of desolation
And a glory that shines upon our tears.

They went with songs to the battle, they were young,
Straight of limb, true of eye, steady and aglow.
They were staunch to the end against odds uncounted,
They fell with, their faces to the foe.

They shall grow not old, as we that are left grow old:
Age shall not weary them, nor the years condemn.
At the going down of the sun and in the morning
We will remember them.

They mingle not with their laughing comrades again;
They sit no more at familiar tables of home;
They have no lot in our labour of the day-time;
They sleep beyond England's foam.

But where our desires are and our hopes profound,
Felt as a well-spring that is hidden from sight,
To the innermost heart of their own land they are known
As the stars are known to the Night;

As the stars that shall be bright when we are dust,
Moving in marches upon the heavenly plain,
As the stars that are starry in the time of our darkness,
To the end, to the end, they remain.

THE BEREAVED

We grudged not those that were dearer than all we possessed,
Lovers, brothers, sons.
Our hearts were full, and out of a full heart
We gave our beloved ones.

Because we loved, we gave. In the hardest hour
When at last — so much unsaid
In the eyes — they went, simply, with tender smile,

Our hearts to the end they read.

They to their deeds! To things that their soul hated
And yet to splendours won
From smoking bell by the spirit that moved in them;
But we to endure alone.

Their hearts rested on ours; their homing thoughts
Met ours in the still of the night.
We ached with the ache of the long waiting, and throbbed
With the throbs of the surging fight.

O had we failed them, then were we desolate now
And separated indeed.
What should have comforted, what should have helped us then
In the time of our bitter need!

But now, though sorrow be ever fresh, sorrow
Is tender as love; it knows
That of love it was born, and Love with the shining eyes
The hard way chose.

And out of deeps eternal, night and day,
A strength our sorrow frees,
Flooding us, full as the tide up the rivers flows
From the depth of the silent seas,

A strength that is mightier far than we, yet a strength
Whereof our spirit is breath,
Hope of the world, that is strange to hazard and fear,
And the wounds of Time, and Death.

STRANGE FRUIT

This year the grain is heavy-ripe;
The apple shows a ruddier stripe;
Never berries so profuse
Blackened with so sweet a juice
On brambly hedges, summer-dyed
The yellow leaves begin to glide;
But Earth in careless lap-ful treasures
Pledge of over-brimming measures.
As if some rich unwonted zest
Stirred prodigal within her breast.
And now, while plenty 's left uncared,
The fruit unplucked, the sickle spared,

Where men go forth to waste and spill,
Toiling to burn, destroy, and kill,
Lo, also side by side with these
Beast-hungers, ravening miseries,
The heart of man has brought to birth
Splendours richer than his earth.
Now in the thunder-hour of fate
Each one is kinder to his mate;
The surly smile; the hard forbear;
There 's help and hope for all to share;
And sudden visions of good-will,
Transcending all the scope of ill,
Like a glory of rare weather
Link us in common light together,
A clearness of the cleansing sun,
Where none 's alone and all are one;
And touching each a priceless pain
We find our own true hearts again.
No more the easy masks deceive:
We give, we dare, and we believe.

THE HARVEST

Red reapers under these sad August skies,
Proud War-Lords, careless of ten thousand dead,
Who leave earth's kindly crops unharvested
As you have left the kindness of the wise
For brutal menace and for clumsy lies,
The spawn of insolence by bragging fed,
With power and fraud in faith's and honour's stead,
Accounting these but good stupidities;

You reap a heavier harvest than you know.
Disnaturing a nation, you have thieved
Her name, her patient genius, while you thought
To fool the world and master it. You sought
Reality. It comes in hate and woe.
In the end you also shall not be deceived.

THE NEW IDOL

Magnificent the Beast! Look in the eyes
Of the fell tiger towering on his prey,
Beautiful in his power to pounce and slay

And effortless in action. He denies
All but himself. He gloats on his weak prize,
Roaring the anger of wild beast at bay,
Blank anger like an element whose way
Is mere annihilation! Terrible eyes!

But there is one more to be feared, who can
Escape the prison of his own wrath; whose will
Lives beyond life; who smiles with quiet lips;
Most terrible because most tender, Man, —
Not only uncowed but irresistible
When the cause fires him to the finger-tips.

THE CAUSE

Out of these throes that search and sear
What is it so deep arises in us
Above the shaken thoughts of fear, —
Whatever thread the Fates may spin us, —
Above the horror that would drown
And tempest that would strike us down?

It is to stand in cleansing light,
The cloud of dullard habit lifted,
To use a certainty of sight
And breathe an air by peril sifted,
The things that once we deemed of price
Consumed in smoke of sacrifice.

It is to feel the world we knew
Changed to a wonder past our knowing;
The grass, the trees, the skiey blue,
The very stones are inly glowing
With something infinite behind
These shadows, ardently divined.

We went our ways; each bosom bore
Its spark of separate desire;
But each now kindles to the core
With faith from this transfusing fire,
Whereto our inmost longings run
To be made infinitely one

With that which nothing can destroy,
Which lives when all is crushed and taken,
The home of dearer than our joy,

By all save by the soul forsaken, —
The soul that strips her clean of care
Because she breathes her native air,

Yet not in scorn of lovely earth
And human sweetness born of living,
For these are grown of dearer worth,
A gift more precious in the giving,
Since through this raiment's hues and lines
The glory of the spirit shines.

Faces of radiant youth, that go
Like rivers singing to the sea!
You count no careful cost; you know;
Of that far secret you are free;
And life in you its splendour spending
Sings the stars' song that has no ending.

TO THE BELGIANS

O race that Caesar knew,
That won stern Roman praise.
What land not envies you
The laurel of these days?

You built your cities rich
Around each towered hall, —
Without, the statued niche,
Within, the pictured wall.

Your ship-thronged wharves, your marts
With gorgeous Venice vied.
Peace and her famous arts
Were yours: though tide on tide

Of Europe's battle scourged
Black field and reddened soil,
From blood and smoke emerged
Peace and her fruitful toil.

Yet when the challenge rang,
"The War-Lord comes; give room!"
Fearless to arms you sprang
Against the odds of doom.

Like your own Damien

Who sought that lepers' isle
To die a simple man
For men with tranquil smile,

So strong in faith you dared
Defy the giant, scorn
Ignobly to be spared,
Though trampled, spoiled, and torn,

And in your faith arose
And smote, and smote again,
Till those astonished foes
Reeled from their mounds of slain,

The faith that the free soul,
Untaught by force to quail,
Through fire and dirge and dole
Prevails and shall prevail.

Still for your frontier stands
The host that knew no dread,
Your little, stubborn land's
Nameless, immortal dead.

LOUVAIN

I

It was the very heart of Peace that thrilled
In the deep minster-bell's wide-throbbing sound
When over old roofs evening seemed to build
Security this world has never found.

Your cloister looked from Caesar's rampart, high
O'er the fair city: clustered orchard-trees
Married their murmur with the dreaming sky.
It was the house of lore and living peace.

And there we talked of youth's delightful years
In Italy, in England. Now, O Friend,
I know not if I speak to living ears
Or if upon you too is come the end.

Peace is on Louvain; dead peace of spilt blood
Upon the mounded ashes where she stood.

II

But from that blood, those ashes there arose
Not hoped-for terror cowering as it ran,
But divine anger flaming upon those
Defamers of the very name of man,

Abortions of their blind hyena-creed,
Who for " protection " of their battle-host
Against the unarmed of them they had made to bleed,
Whose hearts they had tortured to the uttermost

Without a cause, past pardon, fired and tore
The towers of fame and beauty, while they shot
And butchered the defenceless in the door.
But History shall hang them high, to rot

Unburied, in the face of times unborn,
Mankind's abomination and last scorn.

ORPHANS OF FLANDERS

Where is the land that fathered, nourished, poured
The sap of a strong race into your veins,
Land of wide tilth, of farms and granaries stored,
Of old towers chiming over peaceful plains?

It is become a vision, barred away
Like light in cloud, a memory and belief.
On those lost plains the Glory of yesterday
Builds her dark towers for the bells of Grief.

It is become a splendour-circled name
For all the world; a torch against the skies
Burns on that blood-spot, the unpardoned shame
Of them that conquered: but your homeless eyes

See rather some brown pond by a white wall,
Red cattle crowding in the rutty lane,
A garden where the hollyhocks were tall
In the Augusts that shall never be again.

There your thoughts cling as the long-thrusting root
Clings in the ground; your orphaned hearts are there.
O mates of sunburnt earth, your love is mute

But strong like thirst and deeper than despair.

You have endured what pity can but grope
To feel: into that darkness enters none.
We have but hands to help; yours is the hope
Whose courage rises silent with the sun.

TO GOETHE

Goethe, who saw and who foretold
A world revealed
New-springing from its ashes old
On Valmy field,

When Prussia's sullen hosts retired
Before the advance
Of ragged, starved, but freedom-fired
Soldiers of France;

If still those clear, Olympian eyes
Through smoke and rage
Your ancient Europe scrutinize,
What think you, Sage?

Are these the armies of the Light
That seek to drown
The light of lands where freedom's fight
Has won renown?

Will they blot also out your name
Because you praise
All works of men that shrine the flame
Of beauty's ways,

Wherever men have proved them great,
Nor, drunk with pride,
Saw but a single swollen State
And naught beside,

Nor dreamed of drilling Europe's mind
With threat and blow
The way professors have designed
Genius should go?

Or shall a people rise at length
And see, and shake

The fetters from its giant strength,
And grandly break

This pedantry of feud and force,
To man untrue,
Thundering and blundering on its course
To death and rue?

On the road to Ypres, on the long road,
Marching strong,
We 'll sing a song of Ypres, of her glory
And her wrong.

Proud rose her towers in the old time,
Long ago.
Trees stood on her ramparts, and the water
Lay below.

Shattered are the towers into potsherds —
Jumbled stones.
Underneath the ashes that were rafters
Whiten bones.

Blood is in the cellar where the wine was,
On the floor.
Rats run on the pavement where the wives met
At the door.

But in Ypres there 's an army that is biding,
Seen of none.
You 'd never hear their tramp nor see their shadow
In the sun.

Thousands of the dead men there are waiting
Through the night,
Waiting for a bugle in the cold dawn
Blown for fight.

Listen when the bugle 's calling Forward!
They 'll be found,
Dead men, risen in battalions
From underground,

Charging with us home, and through the foe-men

Driving fear
Swifter than the madness in a madman,
As they hear

Dead men ring the bells of Ypres
For a sign,
Hear the bells and fear them in the Hunland
Over Rhine!

AT RHEIMS

Their hearts were burning in their breasts
Too hot for curse or cries.
They stared upon the towers that burned
Before their smarting eyes.

There where, since France began to be,
Anointed kings knelt down,
There where the Maid, the unafraid,
Received her vision's crown,

The senseless shell with nightmare scream
Burst, and fair fragments fell
Torn from their centuries of peace
As by the rage of hell.

What help for wrath, what use for wail?
Before a dumb despair
All ancient, high, heroic France
Seemed burning, bleeding there.

Within, the pillars soar to gloom
Lit by the glimmering Rose;
Spirits of beauty shrined in stone
Afar from mortal woes,

Hearing not, though their haunted shade
Is stricken, and all around
With splintering flash and brutal crash
The ghostly aisles resound.

And there, upon the pavement stretched,
The German wounded groan
To see the dropping flames of death
And feel the shells their own.

Too fierce the fire! Helped by their foes
They stagger out to air.
The green-grey coats are seen, are known
Through all the crowded square.

Ah, now for vengeance! Deep the groan:
A death-knell! Quietly
Soldiers unsling their rifles, lift
And aim with steady eye.

But sudden in the hush between
Death and the doomed, there stands
Against those levelled guns a priest,
Gentle, with outstretched hands.

Be not as guilty as they! he cries . . .
Each lets his weapon fall,
As if a vision showed him France
And vengeance vain and small.

TO THE ENEMY COMPLAINING

Be ruthless, then; scorn slaves of scruple; avow
The blow, planned with such patience, that you deal
So terribly; hack on, and care not how
The innocent fall; live out your faith of steel.

Then you speak speech that we can comprehend.
It cries from the unpitied blood you spill.
And so we stand against you, and to the end
Flame as one man, the weapon of one will.

But when your lips usurp the loyal phrase
Of honour, querulously voluble
Of "chivalry" and "kindness," and you praise
What you despise for weakness of the fool,

Then the gorge rises. Bleat to dupe the dead!
The wolf beneath the sheepskin drips too red.

MID-ATLANTIC

If this were all! — A dream of dread
Ran through me; I watched the waves that fled

Pale-crested out of hollows black,
The hungry lift of helpless waves,
A million million tossing graves,
A wilderness without a track
Beneath the barren moon:
If this were all!
The stars of night remotely strewn
Looked on that restless heave and fall.
I seemed with them to watch this old
Bright planet through the ages rolled,
Self-tortured, burning splendours vain
And fevered with its greeds insane
And with the blood of peoples red;
I watched it, grown an ember cold,
Join in the dancing of the dead.

The chilly half-moon sank; the sound
Of naked surges roared around,
And through my heart the darkness poured
Surges as of a sea unshored.
O somewhere far and lost from light
Blind Europe battled in the night!
Then sudden through the darkness came
The vision of a child,
A child with feet as light as flame
Who ran across the bitter waves,
Across the tumbling of the graves —
With arms stretched out he smiled.
I drank the wine of life again,
I breathed among my brother men,
I felt the human fire.
I knew that I must serve the will
Of beauty and love and wisdom still;
Though all my hopes were overthrown,
Though universes turned to stone,
I have my being in this alone
And die in that desire.

On board the Lusitania, December 1914

THE ANVIL

Burned from the ore's rejected dross,
The iron whitens in the heat.
With plangent strokes of pain and loss
The hammers on the iron beat.

Searched by the fire, through death and dole
We feel the iron in our soul.

O dreadful Forge! if torn and bruised
The heart, more urgent comes our cry
Not to be spared but to be used,
Brain, sinew, and spirit, before we die.
Beat out the iron, edge it keen,
And shape us to the end we mean!

GALLIPOLI

Isles of the Ægean, Troy, and waters of Hellespont,
You we have known from of old
Since boyhood stammering glorious Greek was entranced
In the tale that Homer told.
There scornful Achilles towered and flamed
through the battle
Defying the gods; and there
Hector armed, and Andromache proudly held up his boy to him,
Knowing not yet despair.

We beheld them as presences moving beautiful and swift
In the radiant morning of Time,
Far from reality, far from dullness of daily doing
And from cities of fog and grime, —
Unattainable day-dream, heroes, gods and goddesses
Matched in splendour of war,
Days of a vanished world, days of a grandeur perished,
Days that should bloom no more.

But now shall our boyhood learn to tell a new tale,
And a new song shall be sung,
And the sound of it shall praise not magnificence of old time
But the glory and the greatness of the young;
Deeds of this our own day, marvellous deeds of our own blood;
Sons that their sires excel,
Lightly going into peril and taking death by the hand: —
Of these they shall sing, they shall tell.

How in ships sailing the famed Mediterranean
From armed banks of Nile
Men from far homes in sunny Austral Dominions
And the misty mother-isle,
Met in the great cause, joined in the vast adventure,
Saw first in April skies,

Beyond storied islands, Gallipoli's promontory,
Impregnably ridged, arise.

And how from the belly of the black ship driven beneath
Towering scarp and scaur
Hailing hidden rages of fire in terrible gusts
On the murdered space of shore,
Into the water they leapt, they rushed, and across the beach
With impetuous shout, all
Inspired beyond men, climbed and were over the crest
As a flame leaps over a wall.

Not all the gods in heaven's miraculous panoply
Could have hindered or stayed them, so
Irresistibly came they, scaled the unscaleable and sprang
To stab the astonished foe:
Marvellous doers of deeds, lifted past our imagining
To a world where death is nought,
As a spirit against spirit, as a liberated element,
As fire in flesh they fought.

Now to the old twilight and pale legendary glories
By our own youth outdone,
Those shores recede; not there, but in memory everlasting
The immortal heights were won.
Of them that triumphed, of them that fell, there is only now
Silence and sleep and fame,
And in night's immensity, far on that promontory's altar
The invisibly burning flame.

THE HEALERS

In a vision of the night I saw them,
In the battles of the night.
'Mid the roar and the reeling shadows of blood
They were moving like light,

Light of the reason, guarded
Tense within the will,
As a lantern under a tossing of boughs
Burns steady and still.

With scrutiny calm, and with fingers
Patient as swift
They bind up the hurts and the pain-writhen
Bodies uplift,

Untired and defenceless; around them
With shrieks in its breath
Bursts stark from the terrible horizon
Impersonal death;

But they take not their courage from anger
That blinds the hot being;
They take not their pity from weakness;
Tender, yet seeing;

Feeling, yet nerved to the uttermost;
Keen, like steel;
Yet the wounds of the mind they are stricken with,
Who shall heal?

They endure to have eyes of the watcher
In hell, and not swerve
For an hour from the faith that they follow,
The light that they serve,

Man true to man, to his kindness
That overflows all,
To his spirit erect in the thunder
When all his forts fall, —

This light, in the tiger-mad welter
They serve and they save.
What song shall be worthy to sing of them —
Braver than the brave?

EDITH CAVELL

She was binding the wounds of her enemies when they came —
The lint in her hand unrolled.
They battered the door with their rifle-butts, crashed it in:
She faced them gentle and bold.

They haled her before the judges where they sat
In their places, helmet on head.
With question and menace the judges assailed her, "Yes,
I have broken your law," she said.

"I have tended the hurt and hidden the hunted, have done
As a sister does to a brother,
Because of a law that is greater than that you have made,

Because I could do none other.

"Deal as you will with me. This is my choice to the end,
To live in the life I vowed."
"She is self-confessed," they cried, " she is self-condemned.
She shall die, that the rest may be cowed."

In the terrible hour of the dawn, when the veins are cold,
They led her forth to the wall.
"I have loved my land," she said, "but it is not enough:
Love requires of me all.

"I will empty my heart of the bitterness, hating none."
And sweetness filled her brave
With a vision of understanding beyond the hour
That knelled to the waiting grave.

They bound her eyes, but she stood as if she shone.
The rifles it was that shook
When the hoarse command rang out. They could not endure
That last, that defenceless look.

And the officer strode and pistolled her surely, ashamed
That men, seasoned in blood,
Should quail at a woman, only a woman, — dead
As a flower stamped in the mud.

And now that the deed was securely done, in the night
When none had known her fate,
They answered those that had striven for her, day by day:
"It is over, you come too late."

And with many words and sorrowful-phrased excuse
Argued their German right
To kill, most legally; hard though the duty be,
The law must assert its might.

Only a woman! yet she had pity on them,
The victim offered slain
To the gods of fear that they worship. Leave them there,
Red hands, to clutch their gain.

She bewailed not herself, and we will bewail her not
But with tears of pride rejoice
That an English soul was found so crystal-clear
To be triumphant voice

Of the human heart that dares adventure all

But live to itself untrue,
And beyond all laws sees love as the light in the night,
As the star it must answer to.

The hurts she healed, the thousands comforted — these
Make a fragrance of her fame.
But because she stept to her star right on through death
It is Victory speaks her name.

THE DEPORTATION

I

In vain, in vain, in vain!
Conqueror, you are conquered: though you grind
These bodies, heel on neck; and though you twist
Out of them the exquisite last wrench of pain,
They rise, they rise again,
Rise quivering and eternally resist
All cunning that all cruelty can find
To mock the heart and lacerate the mind
In vain, in vain!

II

The train stands packed for exile, truck on truck.
Men thronged like oxen, pressed against each other,
With worse than anger in their dangerous eyes,
Look on their drivers, armed and helmeted, —
Then forget all in sudden stormy cries
As past the bayonets sister, wife, and mother
Strain up to them, clutch fingers tight, are struck
And beaten back, but struggle and press again,
Catch desolated kisses, fight for breath
To sob their widowed hearts out in a word
Their man shall hear, reckless of wound or death
So they come nigh him; a farewell insane,
A passion as if the earth that bore them heard
And in her bones groaned! And white children held
On shoulders where the torn dress hangs in strips
Cry Father! and mute answers wring the lips
Of the exiles, in their torture still unquelled,

A whistle screams. The guards drive, shout, beat. Then
An inspiration like an ecstasy

Seizes these women, and they rush to throw
Their sobbing bodies prone upon the tracks
Before the panting engine. If their men
Into that night of slavery must go,
They 'll be with death before them! Prostrate there,
Tear-blinded, with tense arms and heaving backs,
Young wife and child and mother of grey hair
Clutch the rails, anguished and athirst to die,
While over them the towering engine throbs,
Blind, ignorant, deaf , and ready . But you spare
Such easiness of end, you who did this
Which the sun looked on, and which History
Shall see for ever. Though they cling with sobs
To their own earth, frenzied and bleeding, swift
They are harried up; the bayonets prise and lift
And tear away their hands' despairing grasp:
They are tossed on either side: at the engine's hiss
The wheels begin that road which curses pave
Between those piteous heaps that cry and gasp
Helpless, and cheated even of their grave.

III

But something lives and burns
More perilous to assail
Than flesh of bodies frail:
It waits and it returns.
And when in the night you dream
Of the day that you did this thing,
When you see those eyes and the bayonets' gleam
And the shrieks to your very heart's blood ring
As you do your deed in your dream again,
The soul of the race that you racked, to do
Your Lord's command, that you thought to have cowed,
Shall sharpen the bitterness thrice for you
As it rises before you, crying aloud:
You did it in vain, in vain!

THE ZEPPELIN

Guns! far and near
Quick, sudden, angry,
They startle the still street.
Upturned faces appear,
Doors open on darkness,

There is a hurrying of feet,

And whirled athwart gloom
White fingers of alarm
Point at last there
Where illumined and dumb
A shape suspended
Hovers, a demon of the starry air!

Strange and cold as a dream
Of sinister fancy,
It charms like a snake,
Poised deadly in the gleam,
While bright explosions
Leap up to it and break.

Is it terror you seek
To exult in? Know then
Hearts are here
That the plunging beak
Of night-winged murder
Strikes not with fear

So much as it strings
To a deep elation
And a quivering pride
That at last the hour brings
For them too the danger
Of those who died,

Of those who yet fight
Spending for each of us
Their glorious blood
In the foreign night. —
That now we are neared to them
Thank we God.

THE ENGLISH GRAVES

The rains of yesterday are flown,
And light is on the farthest hills;
The homeliest rough grass by the stone
To radiance thrills;

And the wet bank above the ditch,
Trailing its thorny bramble, shows

Soft apparitions, clustered rich,
Of the pure primrose.

The shining stillness breathes, vibrates
From simple earth to lonely sky,
A hinted wonder that awaits
The heart's reply.

O lovely life! the chaffinch sings
High on the hazel, near and clear.
Sharp to the heart's blood, sweetness springs
In the morning here.

But my heart goes with the young cloud
That voyages the April light
Southward, across the beaches loud
And cliffs of white

To fields of France, far fields that spread
Beyond the tumbling of the waves,
And touches as with shadowy tread
The English graves.

There too is Earth that never weeps,
The unrepining Earth, that holds
The secret of a thousand sleeps
And there unfolds

Flowers of sweet ignorance on the slope
Where strong arms dropped and blood choked breath,
Earth that forgets all things but hope
And smiles on death.

They poured their spirits out in pride,
They throbbed away the price of years:
Now that dear ground is glorified
With dreams, with tears.

A flower there is sown, to bud
And bloom beyond our loss and smart.
Noble France, at its root is blood
From England's heart.

GOING WEST

Just as I came

Into the empty, westward-facing room,
A sudden gust blew wide
The tall window; at once
A shock of sudden light, vibrating like a flame,
Entered, as if it were the wind's bright spirit
Stealing to me upon some secret quest.
The wonder of the West
Burst open; under dark and rushing cloud
That rained illumined drops, it glorified
Each corner where so dazzlingly it struck:
The shadows cowered, the brilliance over-flowed.
As suddenly, all faded.
Wet, wild air blew in
At the idly-swinging door
Stormily crumpled fallen shreds of leaves,
Dried scarlet and burnt yellow and ashy-brown:
They fluttered in like fears and blew across the floor.
And I, to the heart invaded,
Felt as that wild light palpitated through me
And died in a moment down,
Exalted by a visionary fear
That from the light more than the shadow fell;
A divination of splendid spirits near,
Of glorious parting and of great farewell.

FETCHING THE WOUNDED

At the road's end glimmer the station lights;
How small beneath the immense hollow of Night's
Lonely and living silence! Air that raced
And tingled on the eyelids as we faced
The long road stretched between the poplars flying
To the dark behind us, shuddering and sighing
With phantom foliage, lapses into hush.
Magical supersession! The loud rush
Swims into quiet: midnight reassumes
Its solitude; there 's nothing but great glooms,
Blurred stars; whispering gusts; the hum of wires.
And swerving leftwards upon noiseless tires
We glide over the grass that smells of dew.
A wave of wonder bathes my body through!
For there in the headlamps' gloom-surrounded beam
Tall flowers spring before us, like a dream,
Each luminous little green leaf intimate
And motionless, distinct and delicate
With powdery white bloom fresh upon the stem,

As if that clear beam had created them
Out of the darkness. Never so intense
I felt the pang of beauty's innocence,
Earthly and yet unearthly,

A sudden call!
We leap to ground, and I forget it all.
Each hurries on his errand; lanterns swing;
Dark shapes cross and re-cross the rails; we bring
Stretchers, and pile and number them; and heap
The blankets ready. Then we wait and keep
A listening ear. Nothing comes yet; all's still.
Only soft gusts upon the wires blow shrill
Fitfully, with a gentle spot of rain.
Then, ere one knows it, the long gradual train
Creeps quietly in and slowly stops. No sound
But a few voices' interchange. Around
Is the immense night-stillness, the expanse
Of faint stars over all the wounds of France.
Now stale odour of blood mingles with keen
Pure smell of grass and dew. Now lantern sheen
Falls on brown faces opening patient eyes
And lips of gentle answers, where each lies
Supine upon his stretcher, black of beard
Or with young cheeks; on caps and tunics smeared
And stained, white bandages round foot or head
Or arm, discoloured here and there with red.
Sons of all corners of wide France; from Lille,
Douay, the land beneath the invader's heel,
Champagne, Touraine, the fisher-villages
Of Brittany, the valleyed Pyrenees,
Blue coasts of the South, old Paris streets.
Argonne
Of ever smouldering battle, that anon
Leaps furious, brothered them in arms. They fell
In the trenched forest scarred with reeking shell.
Now strange the sound comes round them in the night
Of English voices. By the wavering light the air,
And sweating in the dark lift up with care,
Tense-sinewed, each to his place. The cars at last
Complete their burden: slowly, and then fast
We glide away.
And the dim round of sky,
Infinite and silent, broods unseeingly
Over the shadowy uplands rolling black
Into far woods, and the long road we track
Bordered with apparitions, as we pass,
Of trembling poplars and lamp-whitened grass,

A brief procession flitting like a thought
Through a brain drowsing into slumber; nought
But we awake in the solitude immense!
But hurting the vague dumbness of my sense
Are fancies wandering the night: there steals
Into my heart, like something that one feels
In darkness, the still presence of far homes
Lost in deep country, and in little rooms
The vacant bed. I touch the world of pain
That is so silent. Then I see again
Only those infinitely patient faces
In the lantern beam, beneath the night's vast spaces,
Amid the shadows and the scented dew;
And those illumined flowers, springing anew
In freshness like a smile of secrecy
From the gloom-buried earth, returns to me.
The village sleeps; blank walls, and windows barred.
But lights are moving in the hushed court-yard

As we glide up to the open door. The Chief
Gives every man his order, prompt and brief.
We carry up our wounded, one by one.
The first cock crows: the morrow is begun.

THE EBB OF WAR

In the seven-times taken and retaken town
Peace! The mind stops; sense argues against sense.
The August sun is ghostly in the street
As if the Silence of a thousand years
Were its familiar. All is as it was
At the instant of the shattering; flat-thrown walls;
Dislocated rafters; lintels blown awry
And toppling over; what were windows, merely
Gapings on mounds of dust and shapelessness;
Charred posts caught in a bramble of twisted iron;
Wires sagging tangled across the street; the black
Skeleton of a vine wrenched from the old house
It clung to; a limp bell-pull; here and there
Little printed papers pasted on the wall.
It is like a madness crumpled up in stone,
Laughterless, tearless, meaningless; a frenzy
Stilled, like at ebb the shingle in sea-caves
Where the imagined weight of water swung
Its senseless crash with pebbles in myriads churned
By the random seethe. But here was flesh and blood,

Seeing eyes, feeling nerves; memoried minds
With the habit of the picture of these fields
And the white roads crossing the wide green plain.
All vanished! One could fancy the very fields
Were memory's projection, phantoms! All
Silent! The stone is hot to the touching hand.
Footsteps come strange to the sense. In the sloped churchyard,
Where the tower shows the blue through its great rents,
Shadow falls over pitiful wrecked graves,
And on the gravel a bare-headed boy,
Hands in his pockets, with brown absent eyes,
Whistles the Marseillaise: To Arms, To Arms!
There is no other sound in the bright air.
It is as if they heard under the grass,
The dead men of the Marne, and their thin voice
Used those young lips to sing it from their graves,
The song that sang a nation into arms.
And far away to the listening ear in the silence
Like remote thunder throb the guns of France.

Maurupt, 1915

LA PATRIE

Through storm-blown gloom the subtle light persists.
Shapes of tumultuous, ghostly cloud appear,
Trailing a dark shower from hill-drenching mists;
Dawn, desolate in majesty, is here.

But ere the wayside trees show leaf and form,
Invisible larks in all the air around
Ripple their songs up through the gloom and storm,
As if the foiled light had won wings of sound.

A wounded soldier on his stretcher waits
His turn for the ambulance, by the glimmering rails.
He is wrapt in a rough brown blanket like his mates;
And over him dawn broadens, the cloud pales.

Muscular, swart, bearded, and quite still,
He lies, too tired to think, to wonder. Drops
From a leaf fall by him. For spent nerve and will
The world of shattering and stunned effort stops.

He feels the air, song-thrilled and fresh and dim,
And close about him smells the rainy soil.

It is ever-living Earth recovers him,
Friend and companion of old, fruitful toil.

He is patient with her patience. Hurt, he takes
Strength from her rooted, still tenacities.
Her will to heal, that secretly re-makes
Like slumber, holds his dark, contented eyes.

For she, though — never reckoning of the cost —
Full germs of all profusion she prepares,
Knows tragic hours, too, parching famine, frost
And wreck; and in her children's hurt she shares.

Build what we may, house us in lofty mind's
Palaces, wean the fine-wrought spirit apart,
Earth touches where the fibre throbs, and winds
The threads about us of her infinite heart.

And some dear ground with its own changing sky,
As if it were our feeling flesh, is wrought
Into the very body's dignity
And private colour of least conscious thought.

O when the loud invader burned and bruised
This ordered land's old kindness, with brute blows
Shamed and befouled and plundered and abused,
Was it not Earth that in her soldier rose

And armed him, terrible and simple? He
Takes his wound, mute as Earth is, yet as strong.
The funeral clouds trail, wet wind shakes the tree,
But all the wild air of the dawn is song.

Latrecy, 1916

THE DISTANT GUNS

Negligently the cart-track descends into the valley;
The drench of the rain has passed, and the clover breathes;
Scents are abroad; in the valley a mist whitens
Along the hidden river, where the evening smiles.
The trees are asleep, their shadows are longer and longer,
Melting blue in the tender twilight; above,
In a pallor barred with lilac and ashen cloud
Delicate as a spirit the young moon brightens;
And, distant, a bell intones the hour of peace

Where roofs of the village, grey and red, cluster
In leafy dimness. Peace, old as the world!
The crickets, shrilling in the high, wet grass,
And gnats clouding upon the frail wild roses,
Murmur of you. But hark! like a shudder upon the air
Ominous and alien, knocking on the farther hills
As with airy hammers, the ghosts of terrible sound —
Guns! From afar they are knocking on human hearts
Everywhere over the silent evening country,
Knocking with fear and dark presentiment.
Only
The moon's beauty, where no life or joy is,
Brightening softly and seeing nothing, has peace.

Arc-en-Barrois, 1916

MEN OF VERDUN

There are five men in the moonlight
That by their shadows stand.
Three hobble humped on crutches,
And two lack each a hand.

Frogs somewhere near the roadside
Chorus their chant absorbed:
But a hush breathes out of the dream-light
That far in heaven is orbed.

It is gentle as sleep falling
And wide as thought can span,
The ancient peace and wonder
That brims the heart of man.

Beyond the hills it shines now
On no peace but the dead,
On reek of trenches thunder-shocked,
Tense fury of wills in wrestle locked,
A chaos crumbled red!

The five men in the moonlight
Chat, joke, or gaze apart.
They talk of days and comrades,
But each one hides his heart.

They wear clean cap and tunic
As when they went to war;

A gleam comes where the medal 's pinned;
But they will fight no more.

The shadows maimed and antic
Gesture and shape distort,
Like mockery of a demon dumb
Out of the hell-din whence they come
That dogs them for his sport:

But as if dead men were risen
And stood before me there
With a terrible fame about them blown
In beams of spectral air,

I see them now, transfigured
As in a dream, dilate
Fabulous with the Titan-throb
Of battling Europe's fate.

For history 's hushed before them,
And legend flames afresh;
Verdun, the name of thunder,
Is written on their flesh.

ENGLAND'S POET

To other voices, other majesties,
Removed this while, Peace shall resort again.
But he was with us in our darkest pain
And stormiest hour: his faith royally dyes
The colours of our cause; his voice replies
To all our doubt, dear spirit! heart and vein
Of England's old adventure! his proud strain
Rose from our earth to the sea-breathing skies.

Even over chaos and the murdering roar
Comes that world-winning music, whose full stops
Sounded all man, the bestial and divine;
Terrible as thunder, fresh as April drops.
He stands, he speaks, the soul-transfigured sign
Of all our story, on the English shore.

THE SIBYLS

Rending the waters of a night unknown
The ship with tireless pulses bore me,
On the shadowy deck musing late and lone,
Over waste ocean.

The rustling of the cordage in the dewy wind
And the sound of idle surges
Falling prolonged and for ever again upthrown
Drowsed me; I slept, I dreamed.

Out of the seas that streamed
In ghostly turbulence moving and glimmering about me
I saw the rising of vast and visionary forms.

Like clouds, like continents of cloud, they rose,
August as the shape of storms
In the silence before the thunder, or of mountains
Alone in a sky of sunken light: they rose
Slowly, with shrouded grandeur

Of queenly bosom and shoulder; and afar
Their countenances were lifted, although veiled,
Although heavy as with thought and with silence,
In the heights where dimly gathered
Star upon solitary star.

And it seemed to me, as I dreamed,
That these were the forms of the Sibyls of old,
Prophetesses whose eyes were aflame with interior fire,
Who passionately prophesied and none comprehended,
In the womb of whose thought was quickened the world's desire,
Who saw, and because they saw, chastised
With voices terribly chanting on the wind
The folly of the faithlessness of men.

But not as they haunted then
In cavernous and wild places,
Each inaccessibly sequestered
And sought with furtive steps
Through wizard leaves of whispering laurel feared,
Now to me they appeared.
But rather like Queens of fabulous dominion.
Like Queens, voices of a voiceless people,
Queens of old time, with aweing faces,
With burdened brows but with proud eyes,
Assembled in solemn parley, to shape
Futurity and the nations' glory and doom,
They were met in the night together.

And lo! beneath them
The immeasurable circle of the gloom .
Phantasmally disclosed
In apparition all the coasts of the world,
Veined with rivers afar to the frozen mountains.
And I saw the shadow of maniac Death
Like a reveller there stagger glutted and gloating.
I saw murdered cities
That raised like a stiffened arm
One blackened tower to heaven; I saw
Processions of the homeless crawling into the distances;

And sullen leagues of interminable battle;
And peoples arming afar; the very earth,
The very bowels of the earth infected
With the rages and the agonies of men.
For a moment the vision gleamed, and then was gone.
Gloom rushed down like rain.
But out of the midst of the darkness
My flesh was aware of a sound,
The peopled sound of moving millions
And the voices of human pain.

I lifted my gaze to the Sibyls,
The Sibyls of the Continents, where they rose
Looking one on another.
Ancestral Asia, mother of musing mind,
Was there; and over against her
Towered in the gates of the West a shape
Of youth gigantic, troubled and vigilant;
Patient with eager dumbness in dark eyes,
Africa rose; and ardent out of the South
The youngest of those great sisters; and proud,
With fame upon her for mantle, and regal-browed,
The stature of Europe old.
It seemed they listened to the murmur
Of the anguished lands beneath them
In sombre reverberation rising and upward rolled.
Everywhere battle and arming for battle,
Famine and torture, odour of burning and blood,
Doubt, hatred, terror,
Rage and lamenting!

I heard sweet Pity crying between the earth and sky:
But who had leisure for her call? or who hearkened to her cry?
Not with our vision, and not with our horizon

The gaze of the Sibyls was filled.
Their trouble was trouble beyond the shaping of our fear,
Their hope full-sailed upon oceans beyond our ken;
Their thoughts were the thoughts that build
Towers for the dawn unseen.

But nearer than ever before
They drew to each other, sister to shrouded sister,
Queen to superb Queen.
What counsel took they together? or what word
Of power and of parturition
Passed their lips? What saw they,
Conferring among the stars?
My blood tingled, and I heard
Syllables, O too vast
For capacity of my ears; yet within me,
In the innermost bones and caves of my being
I felt a voice like the voice of a sea,
And the sound of it seemed to be crying:
"Endure!
Humble yourselves, O dreamers of dreams,
In whose bosom is peril fiercer than fire or beast,
Humble yourselves, O desolaters of your own dreams,
Then arise and remember!
Though now you cry in astonishment and anguish
'What have we done to the beauty of the world
That ruins about us in ashes and blood?'

Remember the Spirit that moulded and made you
In the beauty of the body
Shaped as the splendour of speech to thought.
The Spirit that wills with one desire,
With infinite else unsatisfied desire,
Peace not made by conquerors and armies,
Peace born in the soul, that asks not shelter or a pillow.
The peace of truth, unshaken amid the thunder,
Unaffrighted by fury of shrivelling fire,
And neither time nor tempest,
Neither slumber nor calamity,
Neither rending of the flesh nor breaking of the heart,
Shall stay you from that desire."

That sound floated like a cloud in heaven,
Lingering; and like an answer
Came the sound of the rushing of spirits triumphant,
Of young men dying for a cause.

I lifted my eyes in wonder,

And silence filled me.
And with the silence I was aware
Of a breath moving in the glimmer of the air.
The stars had vanished; but again
I beheld those Sibyls august
Over stilled ocean,
And on their faces the dawn.
Even as I looked they lifted up their heads,
They lifted their heads, like eagles
That slowly shake and widen their wondrous wings;
They arose and vanished like the stars.
The light of the changed world, the world new-born,
Brimmed over the silence of the seas;
But even in the rising of its beam
I remembered the light in their eyes.

BEFORE THE DAWN

Blacker the night grows ere the dawn be risen,
Keener the cost, and fiercer yet the fight.
But hark! above the thunder and the terror
A trumpet blowing splendid through the night.

It is the challenge of our dead undying,
Calling, Remember! We have died for you.
It is the cry of perilled earth's hereafter —
Sons of our sons — Be glorious! Be true!

Now in the hour when either world is witness,
Never or now shall we be proven great,
Rise to the height of all our strain and story,
Aye, and beyond! For we ourselves are Fate.

TO THE END

Because the storm has stript us bare
Of all things but the thing we are,
Because our faith requires us whole,
And we are seen to the very soul,
Rejoice! From now all meaner fears are fled.

Because we have no prize to win
Auguster than the truth within,
And by consuming of the dross

Magnificently lose our loss,
Rejoice! We have not vainly borne and bled.

Because we chose beyond recall
And for dear honour hazard all,
And summoned to the last attack
Refuse to falter or look back,
Rejoice! We die, the Cause is never dead.

Laurence Binyon – A Short Biography

Robert Laurence Binyon, CH, was born on August 10th, 1869 in Lancaster in Lancashire, England to Quaker parents, Frederick Binyon and Mary Dockray.

He studied at St Paul's School, London before enrolling at Trinity College, Oxford, to read classics.

Binyon's first published work was Persephone in 1890. Whilst only a few pages in length it certainly illustrated the talents that Binyon would develop as a poet even though he continued to advance multiple career opportunities.

Immediately after graduating in 1893, Binyon started work at the British Museum for the Department of Printed Books, writing catalogues for the museum and art monographs for himself. As well as being one of England's best poets he was also renowned for his knowledge of various arts particularly with regard to Japan and Persia.

His first poetry book Lyric Poems was published in 1894.

In 1895 his first art book, Dutch Etchers of the Seventeenth Century, was published and, that same year, Binyon moved into the Museum's Department of Prints and Drawings.

Whilst Binyon became known to a wide audience as a poet his output was not prodigious. In 1898, Porphyrion & Other Poems was published followed by Odes (1901) and The Death of Adam & Other Poems (1904).

That same year, 1904, Binyon married the historian Cicely Margaret Powell. The union was to produce three daughters.

In the early years of the 20th Century Binyon was a regular patron of the Wiener Cafe of London together with fellow artists and intellectuals; Ezra Pound, Sir William Rothenstein, Walter Sickert, Charles Ricketts, Lucien Pissarro and Edmund Dulac.

His poetic work continued despite the demands of the British Museum and his other interests. London Visions was published in 1908 followed by England & Other Poems in 1909.

His work at the British Museum ensured promotions were a frequent occurrence for Binyon. In 1909, he became its Assistant Keeper, and in 1913 he was made the Keeper of the new Sub-Department of Oriental Prints and Drawings.

It was also at this time that he played a crucial role in the formation of Modernism in London by introducing young Imagist poets such as Ezra Pound, Richard Aldington and H.D. (Hilda Doolittle) to East Asian visual art and literature.

Many of Binyon's books produced while at the Museum were influenced by his own sensibilities as a poet, although some are clearly works of plain scholarship, such as his four volume catalogue of all the Museum's English drawings, and his seminal catalogue of Chinese and Japanese prints.

Binyon's poetic reputation before the war, although built on several slim volumes, was such that, on the death of the Poet Laureate Alfred Austin in 1913, Binyon was among the names considered as his likely successor. It was quite a field. Among the other illustrious contenders were Thomas Hardy, John Masefield and Rudyard Kipling; however the post was awarded to Robert Bridges.

Moved and shaken by the onset of the World War I and its military tactics of young men slaughtered to hold or gain a few yards of shell-shocked mud as the British Expeditionary Force began its campaign Binyon wrote his seminal poem For the Fallen, with its Ode of Remembrance (the third and fourth or simply the fourth stanza of the poem). The poem was published by The Times newspaper on September 21st, when public feeling was shaken by the recent Battle of Marne. It became an instant classic, turning moments of great loss into a National and human tribute.

Today, For the Fallen, is often recited at Remembrance Sunday services as well as being an integral part of Anzac Day services in Australia and New Zealand and of November 11th Remembrance Day services in Canada. The "Ode of Remembrance" is now acknowledged as a tribute to all casualties of war, irrespective of nation.

In 1915, despite being too old to enlist, Binyon volunteered at a British hospital for French soldiers, the Hôpital Temporaire d'Arc-en-Barrois, Haute-Marne, France, working for a short time as a hospital orderly.

He returned there in the summer of 1916 and took care of soldiers taken in from the Verdun battlefield. He wrote about his experiences in For Dauntless France (1918) and his poems, "Fetching the Wounded" and "The Distant Guns", were inspired by his hospital service.

After the war, he returned to the British Museum and wrote numerous books on art; especially on William Blake, Persian and Japanese art. His work on ancient Japanese and Chinese cultures offered inspiration that inspired many, among them the poets Ezra Pound and W. B. Yeats. His work on Blake and his followers kept alive the then nearly-forgotten memory of the work of Samuel Palmer. Binyon's spectrum of interests continued the traditional interest of British visionary Romanticism in the rich strangeness of Mediterranean and Oriental cultures.

In 1931, his two volume Collected Poems appeared and by 1932, Binyon was promoted to the post of Keeper of the Prints and Drawings Department. The following year, 1933, he retired from the British Museum. He went to live in the country at Westridge Green, near Streatley but continued writing poetry.

In 1933–1934, Binyon was appointed Norton Professor of Poetry at Harvard University. He delivered a series of lectures on The Spirit of Man in Asian Art, which were published in 1935.

Binyon continued his academic work: in May, 1939 he gave the prestigious Romanes Lecture in Oxford on Art and Freedom, and in 1940 he was appointed the Byron Professor of English Literature at the University of Athens. He worked there until forced to leave by the German invasion of Greece in April, 1941.

Binyon had been friends with Ezra Pound for a long time, and in the 1930s the two became especially close; Pound affectionately called him "BinBin", and he assisted Binyon with his translation of Dante.

Between 1933 and 1943, Binyon published his acclaimed translation of Dante's Divine Comedy in an English version of terza rima, made with some editorial assistance by Ezra Pound. It was acknowledged for many decades as *the* popular translation for Dante readers.

During the horrors of the Second World War Binyon wrote a poem that many claim as to be a masterpiece 'The Burning of the Leaves', puts in print his lines on the London Blitz.

At his death Binyon was working on a major three-part Arthurian trilogy, the first part of which was published after his death as The Madness of Merlin (1947).

Robert Laurence Binyon died in Dunedin Nursing Home, Bath Road, Reading, on March 10th, 1943 after undergoing an operation. A funeral service was held at Trinity College Chapel, Oxford, on March 13th, 1943.

Binyon's ashes were scattered at St. Mary's Church, Aldworth.

On November 11th, 1985, Binyon was among sixteen poets of the Great War commemorated on a slate stone unveiled in Westminster Abbey's Poets' Corner. The inscription on the stone quotes a fellow Great War poet, Wilfred Owen. It reads: "My subject is War, and the pity of War. The Poetry is in the pity."

Laurence Binyon – A Concise Bibliography

Poems and Verse
Persephone (1890)
Lyric Poems (1894)
The Praise of Life (1896)
Porphyrion & Other Poems (1898)
Odes (1901)
Death of Adam & Other Poems (1904)
Penthesilea (1905)
London Visions (1908)
England & Other Poems (1909)
Auguries (1913)
For The Fallen (The Times, September 21st, 1914)

The Winnowing Fan (1914)
The Anvil (1916)
The Cause (1917)
The New World: Poems (1918)
The Secret: Sixty Poems (1920)
The Idols (1928)
Collected Poems Vol I: London Visions, Narrative Poems, Translations (1931)
Collected Poems Vol II: Lyrical Poems (1931)
The North Star & Other Poems (1941)
The Burning of the Leaves & Other Poems (1944)
The Madness of Merlin (1947)

Poems Set to Music
In 1915 Cyril Rootham set "For the Fallen" for chorus and orchestra, first performed in 1919 by the Cambridge University Musical Society conducted by the composer.

Edward Elgar set to music "The Fourth of August", "To Women", and "For the Fallen", as The Spirit of England, Op. 80, for tenor or soprano solo, chorus and orchestra (1917).

English Arts and Myth
Dutch Etchers of the Seventeenth Century (1895), Binyon's first book on painting
John Crone and John Sell Cotman (1897)
William Blake: Being all his Woodcuts Photographically Reproduced in Facsimile (1902)
English Poetry in its relation to painting and the other arts (1918)
Drawings and Engravings of William Blake (1922)
Arthur: A Tragedy (1923)
The Followers of William Blake (1925)
The Engraved Designs of William Blake (1926)
Landscape in English Art and Poetry (1931)
English Watercolours (1933)
Gerard Hopkins and his influence (1939)
Art and freedom. (The Romanes lecture, delivered 25 May 1939). Oxford: The Clarendon press, (1939)

Japanese and Persian Arts
Painting in the Far East (1908)
Japanese Art (1909)
Flight of the Dragon (1911)
The Court Painters of the Grand Moguls (1921)
Japanese Colour Prints (1923)
The Poems of Nizami (1928) (Translation)
Persian Miniature Painting (1933)
The Spirit of Man in Asian Art (1936)
Autobiography[edit]
For Dauntless France (1918) (War memoir)

Biography
Botticelli (1913)
Akbar (1932)

Stage Plays
Brief Candles A verse-drama about the decision of Richard III to dispatch his two nephews
Paris and Œnone. A Tragedy in One Act (1906)
Godstow Nunnery: Play
Boadicea; A Play in eight Scenes
Attila: A Tragedy in Four Acts (1907)
Ayuli: A Play in three Acts and an Epilogue
Sophro the Wise: A Play for Children
(Most of the above were written for John Masefield's theatre).